We Can Do
Biography

One woman's story of her generation during World
War II and working as a real-life "Rosie the Riveter"

By G. Sagmiller

Edited by Kaylea Dooley

DEDICATION

I would like to dedicate this book to my mom, Rachel (Hinsz) Sagmiller; thanks for teaching me these stories. I also delicate this to my two children, Savannah and Dakota; may you learn from our history.

CONTENTS

ACKNOWLEDGMENTS

I'd like to thank my wife for helping me to fulfill my dreams and the friends who make sure I keep reaching for my goals. I also would like to acknowledge that in my book, "Dyslexia My Life," I did not always show my mom in the best of lights. All parents have good and bad days; this book is about her good days. It shows the times she shared her life's stories with me. Love you, Mom. Thank you.

1. BORN TO ROSIE THE RIVETER

I was born last of my mother's three children, and she and I shared the same birthday. Because of this, we always had a close relationship. Over breakfast, on long car rides, or to pass lazy summer days, my mom would entrust me with her personal histories. She usually only revealed these tales when we were alone, making them that much more special. One such story was of her time as a "Rosie the Riveter" during World War II. Although that was long before me, it impacted my life forever.

Even before the United States entered World War II, several domestic companies had lucrative contracts to manufacture war equipment for the U.S. Allies. When the United States entered the war almost overnight, production had to increase. And fast. Auto factories were converted to build airplanes; shipyards were expanded to accommodate battleships. At the same time, new factories were being built and all of them needed workers. At first, companies did not think there would be a labor shortage. They didn't take the idea of hiring women seriously. Eventually, their opinion changed as more and more men left for war. Women became important in manufacturing facilities and the term "Rosie the Riveter" was coined.

I could hear the pride in Mom's voice when she told me her stories. My mom's generation lived in a different time and a different world. It was a world before the nuclear bomb and a time prior to many events that forever changed society. Her stories reflected those earlier times and allowed me to better understand the people of her era. She gave me an empathetic view of life in the past and how a previous generation saw the world. It is a life that those who came after would not otherwise know. I believe that through such stories mankind can repeat the past's successes and not its mistakes. For that reason, I have also added some facts to these tales, but they remain my mother's words of her history, which I now pass on with great joy. History brings us understanding, and my mother's began in a town called Zap, North Dakota.

My mom was the least likely person to become a "Rosie the Riveter." She was born as a middle child on the plains of North Dakota to a farmer and his wife. There were six children altogether, five girls and one boy. In our talks, she explained to me that both her mother and father's families came to the United States when they were pushed out of Russia.

The two families were from Germany, but moved to Russia and were labeled "Germans from Russia" prior to moving to the United States.

I found that many family stories passed down from generation to generation eventually guide how the later generations react to the world. What follows is a story that will perfectly exemplify that. My grandfather's grandfather was sitting in church in Russia. Church was something the Russian government was not happy about. While my ancestor was worshipping with his family, Russian soldiers kicked open the door. A soldier walked in, strolled around the church, and stopped at my great - great grandfather, placing a gun at his head. The rest of the family was unaware of this at the time; they were singing a bible song with the rest of the congregation. Not knowing what to do, he continued to sing even at the mercy of the gun. The Russian soldier just stood there, holding the gun for what seemed to be hours. But he never pulled the trigger. The soldier left, taking his fellows with him.

As I was told, events such as that one were fairly normal. The military harassed people at will and the immigrants from Germany were viewed as lower class citizens. They had no voices and were treated like dogs. As with all Germans that moved to Russia, my family had many of these unfortunate occurrences with the military. They also could not

speak German or they would be shot. They were
not allowed to eat or make white bread, as that was
only for the upper class. Death would be the
punishment if they were found with white bread.
The soldiers would "check" homes; Mom explained
that they were truly raids. The event at the church
pushed my family over the edge and they decided to
leave, forsaking everything they could not easily
pack and setting out for a new life in America. It was
time for them to go in search of the freedoms of
speech and worship.

2 FAMILY TRIP

The trip from Russia was neither short nor easy. One of my great uncles, who was only a boy of twelve at the time, died on that trip. The ship was getting close to New York, but had no way to store a dead body. It was to be tossed overboard. The ship's hands called it "Feeding the Whales." They told the families of the dead that the whales wouldn't bother the ship if they were fed. My family, not wanting to dump the poor boy into the sea, hid the body in one of their steamer trunks until they got to New York, where they could give him a proper burial.

My mom shared many stories with me about burials and how critical a proper one was. Her family had strong beliefs about burial and how it was connected to whether or not the deceased could enter Heaven. Beyond that, it reflected heavily on how the surviving family was viewed by the people around them. She told me that a man who committed suicide was buried outside of the church's cemetery and placed facing north to south so he could not see the rising sun or the son of God rising to call to him. Families of suicides were forced out of the church, never to be allowed back.

To bring the point of the importance of burials home, Mom also told me the story of a North Dakota church minister who had an affair with someone in his congregation. He was chained to the front lawn of the church so the townspeople could come by and spit on him or toss stones at him. When he died years later, he was not allowed to be buried in the church graveyard. It is that same strictness and tradition that caused my ancestors to keep my great uncle's body from the whales.

The family arrived at Ellis Island to a great crowd. It was a very different world to someone just off the farm. They stood in line for what seemed to be forever. When they finally arrived at the head of the line, they approached the man who was serving one person at a time. He asked for their last name and told them, "Your American name is now Hinsz." He also asked them what church they belonged to, Catholic or Lutheran. My family answered Lutheran. They later found out this helped the man servicing the new immigrants to decide the township where they would get land. The government understood the tension between the Catholic and Lutheran groups and intentionally kept them apart.

I remembered a story my mom told about that very religious tension. When a Catholic married a Lutheran, the Catholic Church forced their church member to sign a paper that stated he or she would kill the Lutheran spouse if war ever broke out between the two groups. Curious, I once asked a Catholic priest about this practice. He confirmed it and also added that some Lutheran churches required the same. Obviously, this was done to keep people in their own denomination.

The man asking the questions at Ellis Island next took chalk and made a big white mark on the backs of my family, directing them to a waiting train. Everyone else that shared their car on the train had the same marks on their backs. This frightened my family; they had no idea what to expect. No one told them where they were going or why they were being sent there. The journey was a long one, during which they eventually learned bits and pieces of what awaited them. They eventually arrived in North Dakota and were given land, but they had nothing else. There they built a sod house and, eventually, they called it home.

3 THE WAR EFFORT

Years went by. My grandfather met my grandmother and the family added my mom, along with the other children. My mother, Rachel Hinsz at the time, had a normal life compared to most young farm children in North Dakota. She lived though the end of the Dirty Thirties and the beginning of The Great Depression. Then, when she was only eight years old, her father died. The family now had to fend for themselves. They managed well enough for the next couple of years, at least until her mom found a new husband. Rachel's new stepfather had three boys from a previous marriage. After marrying my grandmother, this new man took over her family's farm and chased the only boy that wasn't his own, my uncle, away from the land. Mom explained to me, in a manner of speaking, that he had only ever wanted the farm, and ran it with his three sons. Mom never had a good word to say about this man, and he eventually lost the farm. She thought the world of her birth father and missed him with every fiber of her soul. She wished he was still alive to take care of the family. If he was still alive, she believed, her family's lives would have turned out much happier. Instead, they were left to her stepfather's plans.

A Rosie the Riveter Story, a Biography of my Mom

Mom told me a story of her stepfather. He was having chest pains and asked her to get him a glass of water. At that time, there was no running water in the home. It wasn't like today, where one can just go to the faucet and pour a glass on a whim. People had to go outside and use a hand pump at the well. If the pump was frozen, they had to use a lot of physical strength to break the pump loose and pump repeatedly until water came up. Then, they'd fill the glass and go inside. Most farm homes had buckets for water. They'd fill the bucket and carry it into the house, where it typically sat in the kitchen, ready and waiting for a glass to be dipped in for a drink. But her stepdad wanted fresh, cool water. I'm certain that the story of her grandfather in the church came to mind, telling her not to give in to fear, as it must have come a thousand other times. As she got him a fresh glass of water and handed it to him, she secretly wished he would fall over dead and forever leave her and the family alone. She got her wish. He died that day. She never really got over the feeling that she had somehow killed him. Despite her dislike of him, it bothered her that she had wished ill upon him and he had died.

After his death, the extended family split up as they had been before the marriage and went their separate ways. There was no farm left. My grandmother moved to town and got a job cooking at the local school in Zap. She had to pay off some of the bills her late second husband had gathered while they were married. She also had a baby from her marriage to him and now, for the second time in her life, she was raising children as a widowed mother. I never did meet any of the stepbrothers or sisters. They all moved away and my mom's side of the family never had much to do with them afterwards. While my mother was usually in the habit of keeping contact with everyone she knew, this was one of the rare and odd exceptions.

By this time, my mom was graduating from high school. War had broken out and she wanted to get out of town. Her best friend came up with the idea of getting on the train, riding west, and going to Seattle to work in the Boeing factory. In that way, they could help the war effort. I never understood how an entire nation could be moved so much by a single event, even one as large as the war, until September 11, 2001 when the World Trade Centers were attacked by terrorists. That event moved me greatly, so now I can appreciate why my mom was moved by the war. The bombing of Pearl Harbor moved my mom and her generation as much as September 11th moved ours. Just as the story of her grandfather had strengthened my mother and helped to define how she would act, so did prior wars strengthen my generation when we were attacked.

A Rosie the Riveter Story, a Biography of my Mom

My Mom's High School Graduation Photo

My mom and her friend both wanted to do something for the war efforts. Her friend's original idea was to join the army through an organization called "The Women's Army Corps." But my mother liked her freedom too much and, she said, women in the Army had really bad shoes. Again, she recalled what happened with my great – great grandfather in the Russian church. She didn't like the idea of putting a gun to someone's head and certainly didn't want to bully anyone like he'd been bullied. She liked the idea of working in the Boeing factory better. Airplanes were new, high-tech, and exciting. This was how she could help the war effort and be a good American. Society dictated action. Everyone had to do something to help. My mom talked about movies and songs that called all Americans to action. The "Rosie the Riveter" campaign was one such call to action. According to the "*Encyclopedia of American Economic History,*" "Rosie the Riveter" inspired a social movement that increased the number of working American women to 20 million by 1944, a fifty-seven percent increase from 1940. And my mom was part of the movement.

Aside from helping her country during the war, my mother also saw this as an opportunity to help her mother. Each family was rationed gas and food stamps. There were a limited number of certain items for each family. With one less mouth to feed, the rationed food and gas stamps would go farther. So, Mom made her decision and bought a ticket on the train. She and her friend said their goodbyes to family and headed for the west coast. Both had never been out of the state of North Dakota in their entire lives. In fact, both had never been more than one hundred and fifty miles from home. They saw the mountains for the first time and met people from all over the United States.

4 TO SEATTLE

Upon arriving in Seattle, the two young women got a room and stayed at the Cedarburk Hotel. Later, they moved into a one room apartment. My mom and her friend were both forced to look for work; they could not get a job at Boeing. Their first job was packing supply boxes for U.S. Navy ships. As each ship came in for repairs and to reload supplies, the packing crew would get a list of things to pack for that ship. The teams filled the wooden crates as directed. The ship's name was the last thing to be placed on the box, painted onto the sides of the wooden crates. Most of the time, the group did not know what ship they were packing for until the ship hit dock and was ready to load. This was done so as not to alert the enemy to which ships were being pulled from the war. If the enemy knew this, they might learn where holes were being opened on the front lines.

Mom enjoyed seeing the names of the ships go by, state by state as she worked in the Navy Supply Depot at Pier 91 and 92. She talked about packing for the Navy ships named after states. She packed for the USS South Dakota (BB-57). That ship was the closest she ever got to packing for the ship named after her home state, the USS North Dakota. Battleships, by law, were named this way. The USS South Dakota was a battleship in the United States Navy from 1942 until 1947. The lead ship of her class, the USS South Dakota was the third ship of the U.S. Navy to be named in honor of the 40th state. During World War II, the ship served in a fifteen month tour of the Pacific theater, where she saw combat. The ship participated in combat operations preparatory to the invasion of Japan until her return to the United States in October 1945.

On a trip through South Dakota, I stopped with my mom at a town that supplied parts for the USS South Dakota. She really enjoyed that. After that stop, she talked for the entire drive about packing for the ships. She explained how everything had to be perfect. The boxes were not packed by similar items together, but by size. They attempted to pack the boxes to leave the least amount of unused space. My mom later used this skill when we went on family vacations. She could really get a lot into a suitcase! I remember my dad getting something out of the trunk of the car and not being able to get it all back in again. He always had to ask her for help.

The USS South Dakota *Photo courtesy of the national archives*

The USS South Dakota carried the man who is believed to be the youngest serviceman to have fought in World War II, Calvin Graham. He quit school, joined the U.S. Navy at the age of 12, and participated in battles before he admitted his true age. He spent three months in the brig, had his veteran's benefits removed, and received a dishonorable discharge. Later, he fought to get his benefits and awards back. He was able to get everything he earned except for the Purple Heart he had been awarded for a battle aboard the ship.

My mom packed boxes for the Navy for the majority of the summer. Then, her friend received a letter from North Dakota with a contract to teach. Not wanting to be left behind, my mother joined her friend and they returned to North Dakota by train. Soon, Mom was asked to teach as well. She taught at a country school just north of Zap, which she was able to walk to from the home of one of her students, which was where she lived at the time.

One Room Schoolhouse *Photo courtesy of the national archives*

5 ROSIE THE RIVETER

The next summer, my mom still wanted to help the war effort and enjoy big city life. She decided that if she made it out to the city, she didn't want to be left behind. So this time, she decided she'd go with two people. She talked another friend and her sister Eldora to go to Seattle, Washington by train. In her generation, one could get to almost any place in the country by train. Today, people can still get a train out of most parts of North Dakota. She stayed at the same hotel as the year before, then getting into Great Austin's Apartments. This time, she worked for Boeing Aircraft and built B-29's and B-17's, while her friend and sister signed up for nursing school. Now, my mom worked in the Boeing plant famous for "Rosie the Riveter."

A Rosie the Riveter Story, a Biography of my Mom

B-29 *Photo courtesy of the national archives*

The term "Rosie the Riveter" was first used in a song of the same name that my mom would hear at dances. The song was recorded by numerous artists and went like this:

All the day long,
Whether rain or shine
She's part of the assembly line.
She's making history
Working for victory
Rosie the Riveter

She also told me the plant had a camouflaged roof
with fake streets and houses of fabric and plywood.

The Plant is under the darker part of this photo,
under the camouflaged roof. *Photo courtesy of the national
archives*

Mom also told me that while she worked in multiple
parts of the plant, she started out as a rivet holder.
She'd get a hot bucket of rivets, go inside the plane,
and hold them in place while someone on the
outside of the plane hit them. Every night when she
went home, her ears would ring for hours. It was
very loud being in that plane when someone was
pounding rivets from the outside. I think she did lose

a lot of her hearing while doing this job. She'd always have trouble hearing us when we talked, especially when she wasn't able to see our mouths. Later in life, she needed hearing aids.

Mom was one of the youngest women working on her team. They all called her "Kid." Most of the other women she worked with had husbands in the war. Some had husbands that would never come back alive. I remember her telling me a story about one woman she worked with who lost her husband. She never came back to work and the manager explained that her husband had gotten killed. The lady quit and went back home to be with her mother.

The other women at the factory worked there because they wanted to help, but many did so because they needed a way to pass the time while waiting for their husbands to come home from war. They also had bills to pay and needed to support themselves. And so, they got a job building war planes. Only half of the plane was constructed at my mother's location. She said, "That way, if the plant got bombed, they'd only lose half of the planes and one plant!" The other half of the planes were built in the midwestern United States. A third airplane plant, as she understood it, assembled the two halves together.

My mom spoke of working on the B-17 "Flying Fortress" planes. She talked about being inside of the plane and how it was made. She knew it better than her own hand. She even knew how many rivets went into the key parts of the plane.

B-17 *Photo courtesy of the national archives*

She shared stories about putting the rivets in the pre-drilled holes, hammering them in, and having them inspected. If the team put the rivets in even a little out of place, the inspector, a grumpy old lady who hated the young unmarried girls, would be very rude to them. She hated the young girls who worked in the factory, believing the jobs should go to married women whose husbands were in the war, women who had children to feed. My mother explained to me that she mouthed off to the inspector and said, "Send them over! They can have this job!" The plant was always hiring. If the inspector did not approve of the work, she would have the workers drill out the rivets and start over. It was difficult, time consuming work. My mother hated it. After my mom's comment, she had to spend an entire day drilling out and putting all the rivets back into the same holes as payback.

The days were long at the Boeing plant. It was hot and very noisy. When I was older, I found out about what Mom did with her free time and the money she made while working there. She loved to dance, as most women of that time did. Up to this point, most sports or activities were just for men, but dancing was the one physical activity that everyone could do. World War II changed a lot of things, but every town across America had a dance hall. It was the end-all of what to do for fun. Even Zap, North Dakota, with its population of about 300 people, had a dance hall. It was a place where people got together, listened to big band music, and danced. She explained to me when I was growing up that she felt badly for my generation. She was sorry that my generation did not have a similar hobby. We had nothing to do.

Mom also loved high heels and putting them on to cut a rug. Back in Zap, most of the men her age were gone to war. She had no one to dance with. But in Seattle, with the ships coming in to reload supplies, the town was hopping with other young women she could dance with. The only problem was that she was too young to get into any of the USO clubs or dance halls. Her friend helped her get around this snag by making fake ID cards. When Mom told me this, I was shocked. I was already in my thirties when she told me she had a fake ID, but finding out that my mom broke the law was a real 'wow' moment regardless.

Growing up, the family TV was tuned to "Lawrence Welk" each weekend. On a side note, Lawrence Welk was also from North Dakota. Everyone in North Dakota knew that and watched him as a result. While watching, I ended up dancing with someone whether I wanted to or not. It was household tradition. I never became a good dancer, even with my sisters attempting to teach me. In my youth, I viewed it as more of a punishment than fun or a learning experience. I would simply move my feet until whoever was dancing with me gave up and let me sit down.

While my mom was in Seattle, being on track with the "In" trends was very important. It involved the right shoes, the right clothes, and the right looks altogether. One of the trends that stuck with my mother was cracking her gum. All of the popular, admired dancers would crack their gum. They did this by making a bubble in the gum, folding it in half, and then biting down fast and hard on it so it would make a loud cracking or popping sound. Mom was very good at this. She could crack so loudly and so frequently that it would sound as if there were firecrackers going off. She'd crack her gum when she was stressed out. As I understood it, the women would stand on one side of the room and crack their gum when some man they wanted to dance with walked by. It was a sign for the man to ask them to dance. Later in life, this lingering habit would drive me and my sisters absolutely nuts.

Living and dancing in the big city of Seattle was a huge change for my mom, just as Ellis Island was for the family that had come before her. For someone who had never seen more than a few hundred people in her lifetime, it was exciting to see new faces every week. With the people she knew off to nursing school, my mom met and made friends with a girl her age from California. They immediately hit it off and became roommates. That friendship lasted for the rest of their lives. I remember the two of them writing letters back and forth until later in life, when my mom's friend could no longer continue to do so because of a stroke. One of the saddest days of my mom's life was the day she got the letter from her friend's daughter explaining that her friend had passed away. Mom said that the hardest part of getting old was losing the friends she had made over her lifetime. It made her feel alone in the world; the people that had understood her time, her generation, were now gone. I never met my mom's friend, nor did they ever see each other again after that summer.

Though I never met her, I felt that I knew her well. My mom would read her friend's letters to me. The letters told us what was going on in her friend's life.

A Rosie the Riveter Story, a Biography of my Mom

Some days my mom would cry over the news the letter contained. Sometimes, she smiled. Over the years, this is how they shared in each other's lives. They traded photos, but never managed to meet in person again. I knew every detail of her life, but I could have walked right by her on the street and never known it.

The mail box always had a letter from someone my mother knew. Growing up, I remember letters coming each week from around the United States from her friends and family. She'd write each letter back, but she'd read them to me first. I always enjoyed that. I remember her sitting down at night at the kitchen table and writing letters. It was how people communicated back then. It was how she kept in contact with those special people she'd met over the years. It was how news and special events were spread. Colored marks around the edge of a letter hinted at what would be inside; I never forgot that a letter with black trim foretold news of someone's passing.

Eventually, my mom changed jobs in the Boeing plant and became the rivet runner. She got the hot rivets and ran them back to be reheated after they got too cold. The older women would yell at her, "Hey, Kid! Get me some more!" The noise was soon too much for my mom, however, and she began to get sick of going home with headaches every night. The friend she had come to Seattle with and her sister had long since left. She spent most of her time with her Californian friend at the dances. At one of these dances, her roommate met up with a young man. He was unable to go to war like his friends due to a problem with his leg. The two of them hit it off immediately and, eventually, she ended up marrying him. My mom got a new roommate, but that person stole from her and it did not work out. She moved out of the apartment and traveled to Portland, Oregon. She stayed with an Uncle and Aunt working at the Fred Meyers 5 & 10 Cent store.

6 ROSIE THE RIVETER, WHAT'S NEXT

Many things for women changed quickly at that time. Now, women had their own money and could do with it whatever they pleased. They became more independent. War taught my mom how to stand on her own two feet. With her extra money she could go dancing and buy shoes; it took the feeling of being homesick away when the days were long. The farm girl was now in the city, but she missed seeing the people she had known all her life. She missed the people that understood her and knew of her past, both the good and the bad. With familiar people, there was nothing to explain. She was getting anxious to go back home.

Mom had a fair time working for the Fred Meyer chain of stores. She always got a kick out of stopping at one of those stores whenever we traveled. She worked there until, one day when a woman walked in, picked up a pan, approached my mom, and showed her the tag. Not knowing what to do, she asked her manager. The manager advised her that the woman was the owner's wife. He told her to write down the price and put her name behind it. He told her, "If you act like you don't know who she is, you'll be fired." That was my mom's one warning. This made her think back to the story of her great-grandfather, of the soldier holding the gun to his head. She viewed this as a gun to her head. She left and wrote her mom to ask if she could come back home. In her time, parents would do that for their kids. Children could live at home free of charge until they graduated high school, after which they had to move out or start paying rent. My sisters and I got the same deal. This was the family rule. My mom knew that she couldn't just go back home and move back in. She had to ask first. Her mom said yes and called a local friend, who found my mom a job teaching in a one room schoolhouse in North Dakota.

Mom then jumped on the train, came home, took the test to become a teacher, and passed. A college education was not required in order to be a teacher at that time. To graduate from school in the 40's and 50's, a student only needed to pass exams for each subject. This exam was given by the school district. In 7th grade, the subjects that needed to be passed were Agriculture and Health. In 8th grade, it was Arithmetic, Geography, and History. The teachers were also required to pass exams to receive their teaching certificates. A score of 75 was considered enough to be granted the certificate, which would earn a teacher more pay than one who did not have it.

A Rosie the Riveter Story, a Biography of my Mom

Now my mom was a school teacher for a one room schoolhouse on the plains of North Dakota. It was very much like the television series, "The Little House on the Prairie." It was a farm schoolhouse. Teaching in a one-room school meant that all of the grades were taught in one room. My mom had fourteen students that first year, six of them being 6th graders. The duties of a teacher in a one-room schoolhouse were varied. Mom was responsible for making sure the coal was loaded into the furnace in the morning so when the children arrived they'd have heat. She was also the janitor, the nurse, the policeman, and the playwright.

One of her favorite memories of being a teacher was the Christmas programs that the children in the class put on. It was her responsibility as the teacher to plan the programs, thus making her the playwright. All of the neighbors would come, even those who did not have kids in the school. It was a social event. Everyone brought lanterns, as they did not have electricity. One particular year, my mom received a Santa Claus suit and hat from one of the children. A friend played Santa Claus. Then, red crepe paper was placed around a desk to create a chimney. Her friend sat under the desk until it was his turn in the program to come out. Everyone was so surprised! She also used her own money to buy Christmas ornaments for the tree. She gave the ornaments to me later in life; we had always decorated the tree together. Some of the ornaments are now over 60 years old. Each time I see them, I think of her schoolhouse stories.

With the money she made teaching, Mom was the 1st woman in her county to buy a car. I still have a copy of the check she wrote. It was one of the proudest days in her life and she was always proud of her cars. One of the saddest days was when she could no longer drive and we had to take the car away. The car was her freedom. It was her key to the open road any time she wanted or needed it.

Soon, the war ended. It was one of the bloodiest conflicts in human history. It is estimated that as many as 70 million people were killed. Mom met my dad after he came back from serving in the army; his friend was dating my mom's sister. They fell in love and, over time, she started telling these stories to her youngest child. That child was me. I now share those stories for others to enjoy. That era in her life changed her forever, as it certainly had for the other women who had worked to help their country. That time allowed her to accomplish more and become more than she would have been otherwise. It was an era that also opened the door for future women to do and become more as well.

A Rosie the Riveter Story, a Biography of my Mom

Mr.&Mrs.Delmont Sagmiller
May 8,1949

My Mom and Dad's Wedding Photo

Mom was the only one in her family to be a "Rosie the Riveter." She broke her own personal mold by traveling to see the world and work in the factory. This drive was her gift to me. She helped me to realize that I can do the same with my life. As I'm writing this, my mom has been gone for a year now. She passed away in 2010, just days before our joint birthday. The same year she passed away, Boeing was to planning to tear down the 1936 Seattle factory famous for "Rosie the Riveter" and the women who built World War II planes. They were planning to tear down the facility where my mom and about 30,000 other people had worked, many of whom went on to have families of their own. That plant had always run three shifts to churn out bombers in staggering numbers. At the peak of the war effort, on a single day in April 1944, Boeing assembled sixteen B-17 bombers. The plant manufactured nearly seven thousand B-17's during World War II. Today, only fourteen of those bombers, less than a single day's work, are left in the world and only ten are in flying condition.

One other important event occurred in 2010. Mrs. Doyle was a 17-year-old girl working in a metal factory in Ann Arbor, Michigan. She was featured on the "Rosie the Riveter" poster wearing a red and white polka dot bandana and flexing her bicep. She passed away in December of 2010. She did not know it at the time, but she found out in 1984 that she had been the basis for the poster. Mrs. Doyle's photograph was taken by chance by a United Press International photographer. It then became the basis for the poster, which was produced in 1942 by the Westinghouse Electric Corporation to raise worker morale. The year 2010 seemed to be the end of that area. It was a sign of times gone by. I only hope I can do as much for the next generation as my mom had for hers.

Last year, a month before her death, I went for a car ride with my mom. She could no longer communicate very well. She usually only said a couple of words at a time and pointed to whatever she needed. She had lost most of her words. I drove her around, both of us looking at the world that passed us by, as we did when I was a kid. Back when she was the one driving. I could tell she had more to tell me, but no longer could find the words to say. I talked about my life, telling her what I was doing. She just smiled, letting me know she understood and was proud of her son. A month later, I stood next to my sister looking at her body in the casket. I thought about how she and dad must be in heaven dancing at one of the big band dance halls she loved so much, with her friends at her side. As I stood there thinking about it, my sister told me about Mom's hard life. My sister must have heard different stories from my mother than I had. Mom had been in seven car accidents, lived during wars, and money was always hard to come by. I remembered her laugh and her smile.

The stories I have written here and working as "Rosie the Riveter" changed my mom's life. She always knew she could do whatever she wanted. I miss her. I miss her stories. Most of all, I miss the things she did for me, even those I will probably never know about. I miss the way she prayed for me each day of my life. The memories she shared with me are alive, and now I share them with the world. Thank you, Rachel (Hinsz) Sagmiller, for taking the time to share your memories with your son. I personally thank everyone who has taken the time to read them.

Last photo of my mom, just before her death in 2010

A Rosie the Riveter Story, a Biography of my Mom

ABOUT THE AUTHOR
G. SAGMILLER

Photo of Mom holding me. Thanks Mom for the memories.

Being the youngest of three, with his sisters five and ten years older than him respectively, he spent a lot of time with his mom listening to her stores. He grew up to be a storyteller himself, sharing his tales with the world. He has written a book called "Dyslexia My Life" and a documentary that aired on PBS called "Dakota's Pride." He also went on to travel internationally as an Enterprise Resource Planning consultant for a worldwide organization and moonlighted as a professional model for companies such as Levi Jeans and Anheuser-Busch. He has taught classes at universities and contributes to community services. He serves on many non-profit boards and is the co-founder for one such group called "The Gifted Learning Project." He was also selected for the Family Fun magazine,

A Rosie the Riveter Story, a Biography of my Mom

Points of Light Foundation, and Walt Disney Company's Outstanding Volunteer Award. He was the keynote speaker for seminars at the University o Notre Dame and was asked to be commencement speaker at Maryville State University, where he had completed his undergraduate studies. He believes all of this was made possible because of the stories his mom told him. He was taught that he, too, could do great things.

To Contact the Author, Please email
girardsag@yahoo.com
gsagmiller.com

Me today, with my Daughter Savannah.